DRONE

ALSO BY KIM GARCIA

Madonna Magdalene

Tales of the Sisters

The Brighter House

DRONE

Poems

Kim Garcia

2015 Backwaters Prize Winner
Heid E. Erdrich, Judge

The Backwaters Press

The Backwaters Press
1124 Pacific St., #8392
Omaha, NE, 68108
(402) 451-4052

The Backwaters Press

Published 2016 by The Backwaters Press

Garcia, Kim
       Drone / Kim Garcia.
       ISBN-10: 1-935218-40-9
       ISBN-13: 978-1-935218-40-1
       Library of Congress Control Number: 2016936016

Cover design, interior design, and typesetting by Steve Foley
Cover photo by Kevin Sudeith of a war rug woven by Afghan women living under the drones.
The text of this book is set in ITC New Baskerville.

First Edition

Printed in the United States of America

For the peacemakers

CONTENTS

FIVE

DRONE

BIRD

I set my alarm by an inner dove,
                wake to crows.

Wherever the jay flies
                my sparrows come after.

But above the jittery sandpiper,
                a petrel with a beach of wing

hangs, intimate of the sun, single robin on the skylawn,
                never flocking with starlings,

singular and steady—planet light, hawk gaze,
                heron waiting on the fishrise.

Within that silence, love even for the carrion birds—
                vulture, raven, gull.

ONE

DRONE: PREDATOR

When was I not creating this? these blind machines?

These mechanical—can we say this?—warriors?

All my life I have wanted the bombs to fall

somewhere else. Wanted to dodge the bullet,

skip the hard bits, avoid the crash. This sci-fi

dream, go-cart motor, Klingon-nosed spatulate—

is the movie I feared and willed—lasers, heat-sensing

scopes, inhuman accuracy. Wasn't it us squirming away,

running like squirters, blood black hot, rolling in the mud,

sniped man by man? Don't we remember?

CREECH AIR FORCE BASE: THE NEW ANGELUS

Trailer's cold suggesting a rush of wind,
speed, this room unmanned,
radio controlled. I am only cargo
or perhaps payload, the strike—
these words radioed in from a command
so attenuated we can no longer call
it command, not high command, not chain of.
Just a slow leak, background noise,
the price of this freedom, targets
no longer identified, peace, ditto.

KEVLAR, CARBON, QUARTZ

Too sure for truth, which is cool,
but careful with our bones.

         These weigh
nothing, but glow
in the machine's dull x-ray like silver's
great uncle, white hot.

         This war begins
at the places where shoulder and neck meet
and flay truth to its knuckles.

         Pink roses, blue
veins, then crimson all over and no way to forget.

AUGURY

To read the new birds of the air,
a collection of intellectual property,
mapmakers, eyes of dark glass.

To read the flight paths, solo
and squadron, to observe
all hovering before splash.

To read the tremor between earth
and air, warcraft and godcraft,
and mend with sacrifice the flight-rift.

There is a priestly caste blood-woven
into power, undone by sites as thin
and sharp as a single quick beak.

Black, glass bead of an eye, wing
quiver, early morning song leaking
from beneath any boot made.

The air is still ours to stitch
with winged messengers, living books
not of our making, if we read rightly.

TARGET ID

Like a grizzly's eyesight, not sure until tasting,
   until scent-blasted by hunter or deer
what is meat or meet, what is finished,
   if anything is finished in the midst.

Deer met in mist, the humble gun, fingered
   in fear, three thousand black bags and counting,
already a small town of souls
   giving up self-governance

to rise and gather, condense. I don't know them.
   This is the way I hold on,
saying to the makers of the dark zippered burkas,
   where have you laid them?

DRONE: ANGELS

And the angels threw down the demon

and pursued him and prosecuted him

and drove him down to hell.

Three. Two. One. Rifle. Splash.

TRANSPORT

Between twilight and twilight the muddle-sleep of fear
with a head against a stranger's shoulder. Every bomb
every bullet is coming towards you, every hand holding
a detonator. A jolt in the road, and it's all over. Where am I?
A battlefield is home compared to that place. Then, it's day.

A buddy is sprawled on the bench seat, mouth raw, agape.
Tenderness. Maybe bombs are outside waiting, but here
a bit of morning comes through dirt-smudged windows.
The driver swigs coffee from a flask. He's driven all night
while you slept helpless. A flood of thanks, before thinking,

at the back of his head. The windshield is full of blue sky.
The drones will be out, Bethlehem stars, clearing the way.
You let the thanking in, the melt where fear was, blood warm.
Give in to it, like you give in to the truck's shake through
your bones, like whiskey. Let it soak your parched ground.

DEAD SOLDIER WAKING

                                                    new birdsong
wakes me from a dream about children I'll never have
                                            blankets

cribs with their milky steam of sleeping life the cry I would follow
brushing the plaster with my fingertips
                                            the dark pixilated
with exhaustion with nerves the interrupted cry the hiccupping

comfort the wet blouse the specific weight tipping
                                            as we rock
weight like no other weight particular my empty arms my empty arms

TWO

SEPT. 11, 2011

A mockingbird spreads the feathers of one wing
in the hawthorn, silence after the last pinging
of heavy equipment in reverse;

dread narratives dreaded again;
four black stomachs of fear, the long afternoon;
first us, then them, and them, and them again;

one wing after another, a cloud of shard and smoke
against just this blue.

CONFESSIONAL

That I would see, but not be seen,
that I would have power to harm, when needed,
if needed, it is needed. Harm to stop harm.
That I would not be harmed, that those I love
would not be harmed. That such wishes,
such wishes made fact would be a thin wall
a single unmarked door, from desert beauty
from red and yellow dust and sage-colored
succulents, a powdered palette and the sky
high desert blue in day, stars and distance
beyond stars, and to the west Las Vegas
a cluster of stars half-submerged, perpetual
light an oasis forced out of the ground.
Everything already existed as desire, my desire.
I hover over my enemies—watching—I send out
whistling fire, reorder what I fear, fear again.

HOME FRONT, NEVADA

Driving home after the night shift,
you are the first croaking bird, a shark

scattering a school of air swimmers. Crow, you grim scud
of asphalt refusing sheen, drought-voiced drill sergeant,

even your sun behind a scrim of cloud is a want
of darkness.

      *

Too late the robins frantic
to flush you from the alder.
Too late the three bold jays
determined. Your belly
is warm with the nest's meat.

      *

A dead cat in the road is reward for cunning.
One more bird making a meal of its enemy.

      *

Turn home.
Young crow darken like a bruise
pale blue and red at birth, a nest
of mouth, always hungry. Learning
early to stomach a failing world.

GATE, VETERANS HOSPITAL

for Scott

Among those released, a single soldier
stands with his arms crossed, uncoiling

only to take the next puff of his first
cigarette in the free world. It tastes

like fear, like all the minutes he counted
off come back, hard as bullets.

The road threatens left and right
teases and taunts him, gets in

his face, saying *you can go
anywhere you want, stupid, so*

why are you doin' nothin'? There's nothing
to say to voices in your head. No doors

to keep them out or in. All the meanness
that couldn't get at him is dressed up

in freedom now, walking round him,
getting in those places he can't see.

OMENS

                          —two crows
drink from the bend in the gutter
which never drains. Why call
                          the lords of repair?
They will only fix things.

God from God
Light from Light
True God from True God
Begotten, not made.

                          At the memorial service
only gleaners. More fields sown, more crows,
kings of crow—harvest, harvester, seed.

TRAINS: CREECH AIR FORCE BASE, NEVADA

Trestle, track, whistle. The heartbeat of metal on metal
        trembling side to side in every forward-forward of wheel.

What would I be outside the ring of lonesome whistle?
        A chapel without a church bell. No word

for the long distances, for small towns no more
        than a convenience store, warehouse, coffee stop, pump.

There are places in Nevada where the rain dries up before it touches
        ground, and even Jesus is a thin line of coke with a false high

and a hard fall. But the trains come, word gets out,
        and a man can shelter in a car between yard bosses and beatings

all the way to the mountains of New Mexico, listening to the drone
        of the rail, an abundance of country resurrected in him

mile by mile from the virtual.

OLD FRIENDS

        In my mind's eye poppies, the mountains

of Kashmir, which a poet once told me were the most beautiful
things in the world. He went home to them in a box,

and who knows where he was buried. I lost a friend in Turkey
too. Omar. He would be a father now, not the young boy bowing

and touching his heart, his mouth, his forehead, when he saw me.
He loved the mystics. He had all an idealist's weaknesses, purer

than mind. I would get in a boat and sail across the Bosporus if
my friends could come back to me, still friends, still undecided

about our future.

MAP AS SEEN THROUGH A STRAW

A cold road, a hasp of stone,
a harness, then a leg of brass.

The knot of bone where the hand
once was. Why grieve? It was just

grasping. Children born every day
without lungs, without limbs, every day

and it's our business to call it,
to count. So how long

to will this curse to curse? How hard
the heart is, stiff as rubber tire

stripped and beaten by the gravel
until bald. Back to the helpless crib,

something sweet and thick
suckled from the mattress, muffled.

STATES OF THE UNION

I'd like to say that disaster took us—one fell
swoop, a single ax stroke, a thrust
we couldn't parry. But it was like tooth decay
or the slow mouthing of a sugar cube,
gradual, taking or removing the old
grain by grain.
                              So why
should I expect more of hope? A slow
stutter, piebald, leprous,
waiting on a saint for its kiss.

VA HOSPITAL

Nobody living like this just us not even sandpapered pods making music
done party over late at night the glasses dripping dry listening to tailings
of the conversation ghosting my mind cowboys long views doing wrong
to get right a gold-tipped pin a silver medal the old ways of slipping away
without talking about it without filing a single form just doing it before
the water comes bad water stinking flood drowned all drowned in sand
whole Humvees dead who don't look like the dead look like something
wearing clothes something not a person not anything else like the gurney
rattle when they rolled my sergeant out not my father not even a man
so cold just cells in a shape I recognized that wore clothes that's where
I'm going dying it's nothing to talk about just go and do it. One call.

THREE

THE SPELLING BEE

What does it all mean?

    *That's the question facing spelling whizzes
from across the country, who learned Tuesday that they
will not only have to know how to spell some of the
dictionary's most perplexing words—they'll also need
to know what they mean.*

    —*Richmond Times Dispatch*, April 10, 2013

For the first time meaning
will join mechanics,
third-graders will imagine
the word "mechanical"
and see the gears move
the levers rise and fall.

If they are asked to spell
"prosecute," they will conjure
a courtroom, a judge
and lawyers speaking, the tapping
of the court reporter getting it
all down, making it legible.

The memory hive hums with verbs
that act and nouns that touch
at every point—*drone, nectar,
pollen, wax, jelly, queen*—
where the words touch a world
worth saving, already saved.

ONE/TWO/MANY

> *...all languages have words for at least these three quantifiers....*
> —*Semantics: Primes and Universals*

walking out into the inside of a blue sphere
amongst it

I shrink to a size I can bear, nearly
disappear

driving 95 towards Vegas I get sick
looking through

another window, another screen
stop the car

lie on the ground looking up until I lose
count

of all the things I'm counting—bodies,
body parts

men in a truck, civilians, children,
strikes.

I think *if I'd killed myself last weekend*
they'd be alive

tie-dye blooms of heat on my screen,
warm nights sleeping on the roof

a man and a woman one bright ball—
one, then two, then many.

COUNTING CORPSES: FROM LEONARDO'S "OF THE DESCENT OF HEAVY BODIES"

First: If a power move a body through a certain space in a certain time the same power will move the half the body in the same time twice the space.

Second: Or the same virtue will move the half of this body through this whole space in half this time.

Third (as Second).

Fourth: And the half of this virtue will move the half of this body through all this space in the same time.

Fifth: And this virtue will move twice this movable body through the whole of this space in twice this time, and a thousand times this movable body through the whole of this space in a thousand such periods of time.

Sixth: And the half of this virtue will move this whole body through half of this space in this whole time, and a hundred times this body through the hundredth part of this space in the same time.

Seventh: And if separate virtues move two separate movable things through a given space in a given time, the same virtues united will move the same bodies united through this same space in this same time, because in this case the first proportions remain always the same.

WHAT FEAR WANTS

In the early hour dispatches:
scorpion stings, dislocation, a sand-locked wheel.
Somehow the wary hours pass, orders fulfilled, burrowers
and scalp suckers, sweat between shoulder blades—fear's
spit, hair prickling under the helmet, neck naked, raw.

What fear wants is to clear the ground bald, to flay
itself with shovels, to blacken with fire, to be Leviathan,
earth-shaker and cleaver, dirt-spitter, disrupter and penetrator
intimate with the things feared, the cold sword in the ribs—fear's
sorcery like a cloud at sea, drawing up what it rains down.

TALKING ABOUT THE WAR

while a vet under the Blue Ridge with a red
neck, red arms, takes a battered lawnmower
from his truck and mows the back lawn.

We're foreigners—we know nothing about the land,
where the hornets live, the bog near the ferns,
the root run bald on one side from years of mowing.

He minds it, like he does his own
right elbow—nearly worn out, bone on bone,
a country of aches and pains and poultice.

When he gets home he'll ice it while a face
on his screen says what he thinks about people
on porches who seem friendly enough

but have never once touched him
where it hurts.

DREAM SURVEILLANCE

        I am no longer running.
Who would chase me? who wants to go
there? where the ones I have watched
are watching me.
        We are
in a state almost like love,
almost trance, a hovering—
They are almost dear to me,
my beloveds.
        All is understood
at last. No one speaks. I am moving
towards them without moving,
and they come towards me
        from far off, a heaven
where the past—our irrevocable
past—has been waiting.
        They are patient,
stones without rancor or affection.
I *belong* to them.

REMAINS OF THE SUICIDE: A WAR CENTO

The white hive is snug as a virgin

sealing off her brood cells, her honey

quietly humming.

Bees are flying. What will they taste of?

Maids and the long royal lady, banking

their fires another year.

On warm days, wintering, they carry their dead.

Whose is that long white box?

What have they accomplished?

Why am I cold? A curtain of wax

separating them from the bride flight.

Now they ball in a black mass, it spreads

a mile-long body, the time of hanging-on.

Black mind against all that white.

Neither cruel nor indifferent

they who own me. This is the room,

the room I could never breathe in

wintering in a dark without window.

I have my honey. I have whirled

the midwife's extractor.

This is the easy time.

There is nothing.

Black intractable mind, stings

asbestos receptacles, the smile

of a man of business, gray hands.

How instructive this is:

mausoleum, ivory palace, crotch

pine, the plank draped

with banded bodies, dumb, the last

badge of victory, Elba, Elba.

The box is only temporary, locked,

to live with it overnight. I would say

it was a coffin. I put my eye to the grid.

A mob, unintelligible syllables. How

can I let them out? Small, taken one by one

but my god, together? Furious Latin.

Tomorrow I will be sweet God.

Leave and arrive and there is no end

to the country. Pom! Pom! They fall.

Dismembered. So much for the charioteers,

the grand army. A red tatter.

The bees argue in their black ball,

trains, faithful to their steel arcs,

the beak, the claw, the grin of

the dog. Clouds, clouds, the swarm balls.

Shh! These are chess people you play with,

the mud squirms with throats. Clouds, clouds,

the grin of the dog, the beak, the claw.

It will work without thinking, my honey-machine.

A third person is watching, now he is gone.

FOUR

SURVEILLANCE: A SCREEN LIFE

We will get better at it. The maps we make now,
with their overlapping leaves of sight, stitched
like quilts into a sloppy whole, will blend, smooth,
and we will hardly remember what it was to wonder
what was around the next corner, to fabricate
the future view from dream weave and the past
constantly rewoven or recycled, history re-mattered,
the beach that we found, the forest we entered, the same
and not the same, eerie and evocative. No.
Now, so the dream goes, we will know what to expect.

We've forgotten to be wary of such sight. When we can
read labels on the spice jars in the kitchens of our enemies,
and know how the soup will taste, and feel the weight
of our enemy's daughter resting against his knee, while he—our
enemy, and this we must remember—is cleaning his shoes
or reading aloud from a book we can study from Nevada,
then we are in danger of tenderness, a knowledge that complicates
where it does not disarm, unmanning in its call to husband life.

Just as looking into the womb, the reverse sweep of a windshield
view in ultrasonic glare, revealed a big-headed newt's gaze
looking up with a serenity that bespoke trust we could never earn,
but caught ourselves in the act of giving rise to. What could we do
but fight amongst ourselves in the face of such a witness? What
could we argue except rights and law and money under
the surveillance of beings who could make no claim for themselves?
Who made no claim for surveillance? Reading ourselves into them,
as storytellers do, and because we are afraid, seeking stories
that come out the same every time, inhumanly perfect, machines.

Even now I can feel this poem dragnetting to its conclusion, scraping
up and destroying what it can't speak—the darkness in which the child
floats, the womb and maternal will, a Holy Ghost of consent wrung
out of the story, without which no child wants to live. Just as the story
of the enemy, the way he rises now and stretches his back, pauses
and listens for the truck that will take him to the ammo dump, removes
his longing to stay, his indecision, tendrils of other lives weighting
his thoughts, causing him to decide, just before the missiles
are fired, to nearly stop the truck, make excuses, and head home.
The drone circles his limbs, counting up to a body, weighing
the mass, blocking our view of what we have seen, and who sees it.

PILOT, PREGNANT

In the dream I was in labor. What was I—dilated
nine? ten? I could see it through a scope. I should have been

screaming, but I was walking around, looking over
the doctor's shoulder at my own body, saying I was going

for a run. But I never did. Never had that baby. Woke up
sore in my hips, heavy with a single blind seed.

ISLAMIC SCRIPT

Bodies abstracted, inked and turned
graceful
        calligraphy—vertebrae

into helix. Images
speaking signatures

        under skin.

Those bones dark as lacquer
        released from frames
scroll

a soul, shoulders curved,
        residual
        and delicate ganglia,

antennae tasting the air
for immanence, the hovering
hand of Allah.

Like black crepe twisted more
        always more
around the mind's single
        eye. A stuttering speech,
           a limp.

Or there: the spine becoming blood,
rivering as it cools

around that ink paper already
part of the story—

scholars to whom this book
is always and only true—a day's smoke

sky-twin
absorbing your heft and line.
No name,
you've never been.

CLOUDS ARE A POOR MAN'S ORACLE

cirrus

clear day high
            formation feathering
                            calm seas

cirro cumulus

        flakes
arranged in mackerel
        calm seas

alto cumulus

sheep   thought   massed
  foot   clumped   miles

alto stratus

pull the thick gray curtain,
moon-hides, patched with bright.
Squalling bell weather. A toll.

strato cumulus

blue sky in spools
        twist

dark without rain

nimbus

heart's scud, thick and dark,
small rags, holes may be seen.

cumulus

Heaviest wool pack, alto shorn, large
and various, bright opposite
the sun or dark with an edge,

what a man sees as shielding,
Hannibal's elephants, terrifying
consolations from a beloved, hovering.

stratus

a spread sheet   lifted fog   stretched   laser-thin   a known   horizon   stilled

cirro stratus

halo scrim
        tangled in wires
web-white altitude
        calm seas hereafter

cumulo-nimbus

A headpiece of false feathers,
thunder-twisted features, lightning
flood of mackerel, stockyard pen
of cloud sheep, black-massed
curtain, tangling scud, twisting
under the blue-forgotten lip,
chopping a deadly sea.

DESERT LITANY

Daughters of Jerusalem, don't weep for me—
I did not come to call the righteous.

What did you go out to see?
Daughters of Jerusalem, don't weep for me.

We are convicted by the things not seen.
Will this mountain fall on us? Can hills cover us?

Daughters of Jerusalem, do not weep for me.
I did not come to call the righteous.

Two women will pound grain together, one
will remain, and one will be taken.

Let the mountains fall on us. Let the hills cover us.
Daughters of Jerusalem, do not weep.

Woe to the woman heavy with child. Let the hills cover
us. If you are in the field, do not go to the house.

If you are in the house, do not go to the field. Do not weep
for us. Daughters of Jerusalem, let the mountains fall on us.

THE SEVENTH DAY

the preacher reads *Thou shalt not*

and then preaches it away to glory

not *us*, not now, not *them*. I hear.

The choir makes its altar call,

and I just gotta go, just like last

week, get on my knees, wait

for the pictures to come, almost real,

with tears, almost real, and then maybe

peace. Kneeling until they take me aside

in the preacher's trailer after and say

it makes God look bad, my coming up

week after week, hurts morale,

takes up room at the rail. Don't I

have enough faith to let forgiveness

stick? To remember it? I'm serving

my country, making the world safe,

keeping the troops safe—work talk. I hear.

I wanted God talk, or something like.

I wanted the old lightning to hit me,

and the ground to cover me up, safe, to sleep

with the dead in my chest all gone.

DANIEL REJECTS THE DREAMERS AND THEIR DREAMS

Another saga about Babylon, hanging
gardens, burning bones, drowning
in sand. At the third word, stop,

he knows how it will end—with fire,
sword, a lion licking his salt—the way
friends become enemies, and enemies

bones—the same grim prophecy.
Nothing worth foretelling. A tyrant's
pleasure is a child with a whip—*Tell me.*

Say she opened the door, he turned
in the road, a faithful servant trimmed
the wick and lengthened the night.

Tongue like a tap root, with a scepter's
reach. Fear's dull blade. Grass-eater.

DRONE: HOME FRONT

The fire goes out, no tragedy
in a city stuffed full with heat

and spilled light. Surveillance
smaller than birds, sent with one

intention, arriving with another.
Another administration administrates.

The dove circles, circles the cities
of cloud, citizens of cloud.

AVENGING ANGEL

Flaming swords, deaf and dumb, the all-seeing eyes—
he paraphrases the Book. He is Jehovah.

Every face an enemy to the Word, menacing foreign,
lodged in the secret places—pit, mouth, ear

between evil and evil. *Abba! Abba!* Isn't he the Son
self-cleansing, self-baptizing, shedding baggage of body

and its promises, its terrible yoke—how they yanked him
here and there—he was all soft mouth, they were bits

but now no need of words—these are the last testaments
most pure, each like a blade of quartz. He is

no longer afraid, no longer fooled by their snares, tricky
tight ropes that tangled his old form. The last Book

is opened, his finger passes down the page, reading
the guilty with a flaming nail, searching for a name.

FIVE

DRONE: TOUR OF DUTY

Even here, listening to the birds cupped

and calling in this hollow where cell phones

won't reach, wireless shaky, you can

imagine a womb of earth, a cloister. Even here

the drones like paper airplanes awkwardly

folded, with their blind beaks and albatross

wings, are mapping the territory, webbing

world wide. And we are right to fear

our own fear—its spasms of self-compromise

narrowing life to its straw, pressure

without amplitude, without history and its long

dawn, and tender children always born naked.

I SAY MY MORNING PRAYERS AND REMEMBER
WE ARE INSTRUMENTS OF TORTURE

Home chisels into the mind, and everyone relaxes. They give

you a cigarette. (Now we're getting somewhere.) Trust. You want to cry

again. Thank God, they have a map. There is a pass out of these mountains,

it's only a place. If only you can remember the names, account numbers,

anything at all. Certainly there was money, something you wanted, the way

you want to rub your swollen knees, in small circles of coin, cash in the palm

ticked out like the guard taps his foot, unsnarls the wire, curses you wearily.

He looks exhausted. You want him to love you, to hold out relief, to make

you into sense, so the story they are telling, and now you are telling again and

again, can have its ending. Too late. Too late for him, for you, the village

dark, when you could gently close the book, take the glasses from your father's

eyes, sink into your mother's shoulder, and remember like people with hope.

SEVEN

I'm seven and I can go to hell
if I think of a sin and do it,
so I'm forgetting all I can
but some things stay stuck

like wishing he were dead
even though I said *God bless*
our brave men and women in uniform
seven times seven after

and *Jesus, Jesus, Jesus*
not in the mad way that sends you
to hell, but the happy way that means
you're praying, and you mean it.

And he still hit her and broke things
and there wasn't any reason
but she screamed one time *I'm glad*
you're going back to a Rock

and I'm sure that's bad because he stopped
hitting things and started to cry, loud
so I could hear him. *Jesus, Jesus, Jesus*
God bless our brave men and women in uniform.

And now when I make myself go to sleep
after mama says our prayer, *God bless daddy*
in Iraq (not a rock at all, a sand place),
I dream I'm the girl drone

my daddy said he'd fly one day after he
got done with the drones he flew in Nevada.
One day they'd be drones mixed with people
like transformers, but all good. And he'd

feel his Gs again, and it would be like flying
in your own skin, not inside a box,
and think how high you'd be, way over the desert
and you'd kill all the bad guys and save

the good people. The pastor says when you're seven
you know good and bad, and I could fly over
to where my daddy is and be invisible right
over his bed, and he'd say *Baby, is that you?*

But I wouldn't say anything. I'd watch him
and see when he turned good. Then I'd say
Are you good now? Are the bad guys dead?
And he'd say *Yes, Baby, we're through.*

KINDRED

The hand at work, heart's drone,
map-dance in honeycomb. The path
of flower, clover song, sweet magnetic
north, nectar cooled in flight. River

rocks' remembered wash, a karst of blue.
A sky mountainous with frowning cloud,

stars slipping the city's hot gaze, fastening
their new eyes over fresh yearnings—home

drawn up along the lines of the old ache
like desert seed, fashioning green tongues.

DRONE: THE PILOT'S WIFE IN CHURCH

She wears a kind of doily hairpinned to her crown,

her glory, the pastor says. She stands and the hymn

is sung along with the keyboard, the electric

guitar and the lead singer, heavy eyeliner, a tear

in the voice. The pastor stands at the rail, waiting

on sinners, scanning the congregation.

What should she pray? That her husband's hands

should stop shaking? That he should stop working

on the Sabbath? That he should stop having those dreams,

stop getting up and playing video games in the dark?

Stop turning out the lights and then talking?

Stop not talking? Stop hating her for listening?

Stop killing those men who kill us? Stop killing

those children who cluster around them? Stop

the women who he must watch collect the bodies,

parts of bodies, who are themselves sometimes nothing

but bodies? Stop watching the bodies get into carts,

into trucks, into the trunks of cars? Stop being paid

for watching, for locating, for prosecuting,

for firing? Stop fighting for the insurance to pay,

for the VA to pay, for the government to pay.

What should she pray? How can God answer?

SKY HIGH

Apache country, fog over a horizon that stretches right out
        under its sudden blue visor   simple
                as an instrument panel

drivers dazed
        slightly dislocated as though they'd just blown
                in   hadn't quite   resigned themselves to wind-

slapped transience
        dun-
                colored grass blown clear

BLUE EARLY MORNING SNOW, HOME FRONT

Thick layer cake of porch, trees bare after a wind. The sound of snow
        plow, plane, de-icer, shovel, peach

of sun-rose. A hand raised, candling its fertile egg,
        showing its bud-knuckled bones.

Snow like sky of a steady Bunsen-blue flame under
        a thousand schoolroom crucibles. Fossil

fuel, this slosh of a lantern swung to the shed
        in time to my steps, the surprise of frost-stung

glass shattering in my hand, downed limbs
        I take a hatchet to, the warmth of light's arm

thrown across the pillow of snow, the only thing
        that brings me back, cold, with hot coffee, to wake you.

HOME FRONT, PILOT'S WIFE

In this dream you were taller and very strong,
your arms hung from your shoulders—vast—
and large, heavy like the David's, heavier.

But you were still, too—unresponsive
and helpless in it. I wanted you
badly, nursing at your beauty

making the happy whimpers of suppressed
delight. Even your quiet
precious to me. I wrapped

my legs around yours, warmed
their lukewarm grief. *I will hold you
inside me*, I said. Your eyes

were not your eyes, but
the large saucers of fairytale dogs
in my blue book. I will hold you.

GUARDIAN ANGELS

A medicine cabinet
speaking cures against the body
against blood and stench and sweat
the slow yellow of the tooth,
sleeplessness, against all hope
without repair.
                No shame
in maintaining
the soft warm shell
which slumps and flakes
around its fragile yolk,
small featherless bird,
great, golden eye.

PEACE TIME

like those dreams in which I find attics under the floorboards, secret rooms,
an extra bath with a closet, a window, full of northern light, that opens back

into my own living room, which seems as if it has been closed a long time,
forever holding its breath; suddenly water, quick as grass, returning, large.

Crows come changed as the day cools, pedestrian. They take up less room
than I remember, little cousins of ravens, dark Icari, burnt black by the heat

that couldn't melt them. Water takes their place, and stones, and a school
of quick, silver stitches.

NIGHT FLIGHT, NIGHT VISION

Leaving the body sense, the Gs, tilt
   and recover—what sees?

Flying to the white hot parts of the map
   in mountain dark. Lidless eye

mimicking a god's trick of seeing sinners
   everywhere from nowhere, raining fire.

We are sovereign sight's living hands, dreaming drone-like
   in infrared, grids and pixel-prisons.

Tunneling towards a corps, a vector mapped
   of human warmth, pattern only.

O

Child of the Panopticon, Gorgon's Stare,
   Eye of God, where does your vision end?

CHORES AFTER THE PEACE

The pilot carries out his wife's lavender
blouse, black skirt on a hanger. Rolls
her suitcase (teal) to the car.

           They have made love all day,
trying to imagine their third child.

He balances
the suitcase against his thigh, raises
the trunk, loads her bag, hooks
her blouse, and crosses
the icy drive back to the house

           with the look of a man
who has accomplished something—something
that will wait for him (and only him. Forever.)

to finish whatever he is doing (forever)

and give him something (forever) else to do.

His wife's lavender, the pilot carries,
black skirt, blouse, that will wait for him.
Forever. A child. A car. Something else to do.

The look of a man, whatever he is doing
who has accomplished something.
The car, the trunk, the bag. The child

waiting for him. He balances, trying to imagine,
trying all day to make love (a blouse, a black bag)
A hanger. Rolls the bag. Crosses forever.

Raises, loads, finishes a third house. Something.
Who could have imagined? A child. The car
hooks, rolls, with the look of something accomplished.

Forever the icy drive back.
Forever trying to imagine their third child.
The pilot carries out his wife's lavender.
                    They have made love all day.

DRONE: PLOUGHSHARES

And what shall we beat you into, little mechanical bird

with the head of a bowling pin, speculum, goose?

How to imagine our way back? Rules help: no weapons

in shared airspace, or in the spaces in between.

Then the dismantling, the tidy buttons

on the computer games that kill, yanked out,

harmless like the horn on a Playskool car,

nobody listening, wires dangling and disconnected

from flesh. The leash no longer in anyone's hand,

water drained from the tub. We enter

the Age of Reparations with a quorum of judges,

jurors, journalists. We're everyone—the guilty

parties, witnesses who should have stepped forward

years ago, judges eager to overturn themselves,

and jurists finally disclosing the evidence

they should never have withheld. The judge is stern,

the jurors settle into their seats for the long haul.

They will listen for days, years, as long as it takes.

NOTES

"Remains of the Suicide: A War Cento": These lines are drawn from the final poems of Sylvia Plath. Her father, Otto Plath, was an authority on the bumblebee.

"Counting the Corpses: From Leonardo's 'Of the Descent of Heavy Bodies'": The lines of this found poem are drawn from *The Notebooks of Leonardo da Vinci* (Edward McCurdy, translator), specifically from "Movement and Weight: Of the Descent of Heavy Bodies."

ACKNOWLEDGMENTS

My thanks to the editors and publishers of the following journals
where these poems first appeared, some in slightly different form.

American Literary Review: "Transport"
Breakwater: "Seven"
Broadsided Press: "Confessional"
Brooklyn Quarterly: "Blue Early Morning Snow, Home Front," "Bird,"
    "Drone: The Pilot's Wife in Church," "Home Front, Pilot's Wife,"
    "Target ID," "VA Hospital"
Iodine Poetry Journal: "Kevlar, Carbon, Quartz"
Potomac Review: "Kindred"
Summerset Review: "Drone: Home Front," "Gate, Veterans Hospital,"
    "Surveillance: A Screen Life"
Washington Square Review: "Drone: Predator"

My first thanks to Allison Adair, Susana Roberts and Skye Shirley,
the wise poets in the attic, who took poems I thought of as private
meditations and made them a manuscript.

Thank you to the many talented friends, writers, and artists who
provided friendship and a listening ear at key moments: Kenneth
R. Himes, OFM; Megan Chapa; Emilie Boon; Liza Rutherford; Jim
Henle; the Brookline Poetry Series poets; Elizabeth Graver; Gary
Whited; Brook Emery; Robert Chibka; Jennifer L. Erickson; Chris

Boucher; Lisa Bastoni; Nehal Khorraminejad; Commander Gretchen Helweg, USN (Ret.); Wing Commander Patrick Carroll, RAF (Ret.); Sarah Cassatly; Keun Young Bae; and the panelists and participants at a 2014 interdisciplinary Boston College conference on drone warfare for their comments and insights, in particular to Knuckles, Zoom and Fever for listening with care to poems by an outsider whose politics they did not necessarily share.

I'm very grateful to Jim Cihlar at The Backwaters Press for his careful work, Heid E. Erdrich for choosing the manuscript, and Larry Richman for essential and incisive proofreading.

My thanks to the Hambidge Center and the generous writers, musicians, and artists there who provided the quiet workspace and inspiration for these poems.

More thanks than I can ever express for the gift of my beloved family, Michael, Sarah and Frank, who support and inspire me in all the ways that will ever matter.

And finally to Major Joseph O. Chapa USAF, whose careful readings and thoughtful responses put so much practical sense and heart into the manuscript and whose example as a merciful, moral being remaining present in the face of unbearable choices has been an inspiration to me. Thank you for your service, in every meaningful sense.

CPSIA information can be obtained
at www.ICGtesting.com
Printed in the USA
LVHW07s1937200918
590797LV00020B/242/P